Dream Secrets

Understand

Control

And

Master your Dreams

It's your turn to #RememberTheDream

YOUR ESSENTIAL **GUIDEBOOK** FOR

THRIVING AS A LUCID DREAMER

By Richard Siena

Published by

Alcyone LLC

Bowling Green, KY

270.777.2845

Paperback: ISBN: 978-1-7356384-2-3

Kindle: ISBN: 978-1-7356384-3-0

ALSO, BY RICHARD SIENA:

Learn to Meditate:
Techniques for the beginner and the experienced

(Available on Amazon) 

Dream Secrets website

https://DreamSecrets.us

Rich's website

https://alcy.com

Silva Method Site
https://SilvaMethodKY.com

Dedicated to all those who seek to be awake during their dreams.

How to read this book

1. Don't read it. Consume it. Study it. Devour it. Treat it like a workbook – underline, highlight, circle, star, write, and put exclamation marks in the margins. Dog-ear or put tabs on the pages and bits that have a particular impact on you. Use this book as a daily reference.

2. Implement the key ideas from each chapter with the summary Action Plan and worksheets. You can find all the worksheets and other helpful (free!) resources at:

   https://DreamSecrets.us/resources

3. Share quotes and content from the book that strikes you on your social networks. We've highlighted some of our favorites. Join us in our goal to inspire and encourage existing and would-be dream seekers all over the globe. Please include my social "handle" @RichardSiena, and the book's hashtag, #RememberTheDream.

Enjoy your exhilarating, fun, and wild dreams

--Rich

"Sometimes dreams are wiser than waking."

-- Black Elk

Black Elk (2000). "Black Elk Speaks: Being the Life Story of a Holy Man of the Oglala Sioux," Bison Books

Contents

Chapter 1 Introduction

"A dream is a microscope through which we look at the hidden occurrences in our soul."

-- Erich Fromm

Chapter 1 Introduction

I had a very high, life-threatening 106.2° F fever on my second birthday. It's weird, but I remember having a strange dream during the fever that would repeat every time I had a fever since then. This fever created an altered state of awareness, allowing me to step over to the other side of the veil and experience something amazing. It was a feeling of being infinite but very small and insignificant while simultaneously being the entire universe. This state of mind is a removal of the veil for a brief period. To this day, I can still remember it. I have had that dream every time I have had a fever.

This dream has always haunted me and sparked my desire to understand my dreams.

It was not until later in life that I dove into finding out how to remember and understand my dreams. When I graduated from college in the early 1980s, I came across The Silva Method. This class taught me how to meditate and enter my inner conscious level. One of the course segments was mental conditioning to remember our dreams. It was not a class to teach being a yogi and sitting on a mountain top meditating but how to use the untaught ability of our mind. People like Einstein and Marget Mead said we use only about 10% of our brains. They meant that we use 10% of our brain's potential. The Silva Method teaches how to use the other 90% that lays dormant in most of us. The Silva Method class once again fueled my desire to understand my dreams.

I sought out books on dreams and studied different techniques to aid my dream research.

It has been a fascinating journey that has led to me compiling the best of what I have found into this book. In my Dream Secrets class, I dive deeper into all aspects of dreaming and have guided meditations to help recall and understand dreams.

I hope you will use this as a guide to master your dreams.

Chapter 1 Introduction

The Native American Indians call this Dream Time. They believe the language of dreams and the use of dreams have disappeared in our modern-day world. They consider Dream Time a sacred time of the night when you are in contact with the Great Spirit. The Great Spirit guides and directs you in your dreams. The Dream Language is one of the symbols. Everything in your dream, from objects to people, represents some aspect of you. There are a few exceptions to this that an advanced dreamer may get, but for now, let's focus on them as an aspect of you.

What this book will explore

- What are dreams
- Why do we dream
- What is Lucid dreaming
- How to induce Lucid dreaming
- Nightmares
- Chakras: what are they, and why is understanding Chakras important
- The Pineal Gland and its part in the dream process

Chapter 1 Introduction

- Validating your reality
- What is a dream landscape
- Identify and understand dream symbols
- Archetypes and how do they relate to dreams
- The four elements: water, air, fire, and earth, and what they mean when they show up in your dreams
- Keeping a dream journal

I created several guided meditations to reinforce the material in this book in my online and in-person classes. The purpose of these meditations is to give you a jump start on remembering and controlling your dreams.

You can find more information at

https://DreamSecrets.US 

The meditations aid in the following:

- opening up your Chakras
- stimulating dream recall
- assistance in understanding your dreams
- impressing the techniques

Chapter 1 Introduction

Like you, I have wondered about dreams and other mind areas since childhood. I always felt there was more we could do mentally. We can use more of our minds. School does not teach how to use more of our minds. Religion does not teach how. But when you look at movies, they imply that mental abilities do exist. They also suggest that having these mental abilities is a natural-born talent. You either have it or not. And many researchers believed this also. Jose Silva, who created the Silva Method, was the first to prove that you can teach anyone to use their mind and develop ESP, dream recall, and expand your mind's capabilities. ESP stands for Effective Sensory Projection, not Extra Sensory Projection. We all have this ability. We just need to learn how to access it. I started teaching the Silva Method in 1982 and have used the techniques I learned in my first class in 1980. I use these techniques every day. Taking the course was like finding the guidebook to my mind.

Chapter 1 Introduction

You can find out more about The Silva Method at https://SilvaMethodKY.com.

Chapter 1 Introduction

Chapter 2 What is a Dream, and why do you want to remember them

Chapter 2 What is a Dream, and why do you want to remember them

Chippewa Elder John Thunderbird:

> *"Your soul dreams those dreams; not your body, not your mind. Those dreams come true. The soul travels all over the world when you dream."*

Chapter 2 What is a Dream, and why do you want to remember them

What is your higher self? When we incarnate here on this planet, we go through a forgetting process. We forget who we are and our past experiences. A portion of ourselves comes through, and part of ourselves remains on the other side of the veil. There is a veil between ourselves here on earth and in this other realm. Dreams are where our higher self can talk to us, giving us information to solve problems and find creative solutions to our challenges. Dreams are a kind of loophole in the veil, allowing guidance to come through.

A dream is an archetype situation derived from your subconscious and higher self. According to Carl Jung, an archetype is a universally understood symbol, term, or pattern of behavior, a prototype upon which others are copied, patterned, or emulated. Understanding archetypes helps us know who we are and what our dreams mean.

Your dreams represent some issue in your life that is most important to you at that moment.

Chapter 2 What is a Dream, and why do you want to remember them

Sometimes, it is a recall of parallel lives in other dimensions. In more advanced dreams, it can be prophetic information. But it comes to you to teach you something. The dream gives you new knowledge to work with and understand.

The dreams you have help you understand and work through your issues. When you identify those issues and overcome the blocks you face, you can move on and meet new challenges—opening yourself to an ever-expanding realm of possibilities. As we discover the blocks holding us back, we can work on them, clearing up issues and becoming more successful in life.

Like you, I have had certain blocks, leaving me feeling frustrated and unable to make progress in my life. It seemed like it was pointless to try sometimes. When I started to understand the symbols in my dreams, I was able to relate the symbols to the blocks. Once I understood those blocks, I could move on in my life. Other areas where it felt like I was being held back seemed to open up. I could reach success where success had previously been pulled from me. These

Chapter 2 What is a Dream, and why do you want to remember them
skills and understanding are what I hope you will master.

There are several different types of dreams:

- An individual dream
- Reoccurring Dreams - The same dream multiple times
- Dream sets – a group of dreams related to the same idea

Native American Indians believe dreams give you the complete ability to find your way in life. Dreams open up new worlds beyond a normal comprehension of reality. In ceremonies and the Indian culture, dreams are often more important than our waking lives. In dreams, we experience the shamanic world, gaining insights and information to better our lives, allowing us to astral travel during sleep.

Chapter 2 What is a Dream, and why do you want to remember them

Dreams allow messages from the "Great Spirit" to come to us. Dreams will sometimes initiate us into something, showing us new rituals. The shamans or medicine men of the tribe would get dreams showing what herbs to use for medicine.

Often, the Indians would get advice in dreams on where to hunt or what new relationships to form. They also talked about shared dreams with one or more people.

In one book I read, the author, when he was young, would meet his friends at night in a shared dream.

Dreams are a map supporting and guiding the dreamer throughout their whole life.

Revelations, regarded by the Indians as coming from supernatural powers, were believed to be received in dreams and visions. Dreams bestowed on people magical abilities like the capacity to foresee future events and control disease, giving the dreamer the capabilities to fill the office of priest or leader.

Everything in the dream is a reflection of you. The Dream symbols represent how you feel about an issue, your response to the problem, and solutions to the topic. Learning to control your dreams will enable you to explore new solutions to the problem.

The issue of the dream may be outside of you, but it affects you. The point of the dream is to show you your blocks so that you ponder the content, learn, and understand from the dream. Providing you an opportunity to find a solution to the problem and move on.

Dreams can then predict the future with prophetic meanings when your heart opens. You may experience a precognitive dream if a loved one passes on at that time.

Often, our issues are buried so deep in our minds that we deny what is blocking us.

Chapter 2 What is a Dream, and why do you want to remember them

Understanding your dreams gives you a valuable opportunity for growth by dealing with your issues.

Chapter 2 What is a Dream, and why do you want to remember them

Chapter 3 Sleep Cycles

"Dreams are illustrations from the book your soul is writing about you."

-- Marsha Norman:

Chapter 3 Sleep Cycles

When you go to sleep, you have about five to six sleep cycles per night. Each sleep cycle is about 90 minutes long and goes into different levels or frequencies. Each brain frequency stimulates different body responses. The lowest frequency is Delta, which is anything below about four cycles per second. Delta is considered DEEP sleep. Not too much is known about the functions of Delta at this time. The next is Theta, about 4 to 7 cycles per second. Theta is the brain's level when you receive anesthesia during surgery. It is also a level you can use while meditating for deep self-programming. Alpha is from about 7 to 14 cycles per second and is where the magic happens. Right in the middle of Alpha, at about 10.5 cycles per second, is where REM, short for Rapid Eye Movement, sleep happens. REM sleep is when dreams occur. Alpha is the level your brain is at when you meditate, and it is the level children are at until about age 13 or 14. Alpha enhances learning and, if used correctly, can aid in having a successful life. In my other class, I teach how to meditate and use this level to transform yourself. See https://SilvaMethodKY.com for more on that subject.

When you first go to sleep, you quickly go into Delta, then to Theta, and then to Alpha. Each Sleep cycle is about 90 minutes long. In the first sleep cycle, you spend a lot of time in Delta and Theta and little time in Alpha. As you go through each sleep cycle, you spend less time in Delta and Theta and more time in Alpha. Until the last cycle, you spend most of the time in Alpha. This pattern is for normal sleep cycles. Many things happen during the sleep cycles, like repairing and maintaining your body.

We have some interesting bodily actions when we sleep and enter Alpha. First, our eyes move rapidly. When sleeping in Alpha, we have dreams, and our eyes experience Rapid Eye Movement Sleep or REM sleep. When we are in this state, we dream. The body also puts itself into a state of being paralyzed, so actions you take while you dream are not done to your body. For example, if you swing your arms while dreaming, you do not swing your arms in your bed and hit the wall or someone else.

Chapter 4 Veiling

"Who looks outside, dreams; who looks inside, awakes."

-- Carl Jung:

Chapter 4 Veiling

When we incarnate onto this planet, our spirit must undergo training to learn to be born without knowing who we are. There is a forgetting process that takes place. There is a veil between us in this reality and us in the spirit realm. The veil separates our mind from our spirit. One of the things to work on in this lifetime is to break through the veil to gain access to our true selves.

Our spirit uses dreams to penetrate the veil. Through dreams, our higher self can transfer information into our consciousness. One type of dream includes information on our blocks. Our spirit gives us dreams that represent blocks that are holding us back. By understanding our dreams, we can understand the blocks and work on overcoming them. We can then advance our spiritual development and heal those issues by overcoming the blocks.

In one of my dreams, the message was that I had repressed emotions that were holding me back. When I analyzed the dream, I had no idea what it was trying to tell me. I then meditated and asked what emotions the dream referred to, leading me to understand these repressed emotions to resolve them.

To achieve our goals in life, we need to become the person worthy of those goals. Understanding our dreams can help us become worthy of our goals.

Dreams help us to come up with solutions to our issues. The solutions that “we” come up with are the best solution. Coming up with our "own" solution helps to empower us, allowing us to step into our power. Taking only other people's solutions may not be the best for us, taking away our power. That is not to say that learning from others' mistakes is terrible, but we need to learn to rely on ourselves as much as possible.

Penetrating the veil opens up a doorway to our higher self.

Chapter 4 Veiling

Lifting the veil removes or breaks through the barriers that obscure and conceal the true nature of ourselves and our reality. By lifting the veil, we gain a deeper understanding and insight into the true nature of reality beyond the limitations of our everyday perception and understanding. Breaking through leads us to a transformative and enlightening experience, allowing us to see beyond the veil of existence and gain a more comprehensive understanding of the world and our place in it.

Lifting the veil reveals and exposes things previously hidden and unknown. Uncovering these secrets allows us to understand our nature more deeply. Lifting the veil involves a process of investigation, research, and discovery that will enable us to gain new insights and knowledge about ourselves and our previously obscure and mysterious reality.

Chapter 5 Chakras

"The heart is not only the location of the 4th chakra, located at the center of your chakra system but also the center of your conscious universe and can create and define life in its true essence."

-- Steven Redhead

Chapter 5 Chakras

Understanding your dreams helps with the knowledge of the energy centers of your body. These energy centers are called Chakras. As you start to analyze your dreams, certain symbols in the dream relate to your Chakras. We will explore these symbols in the section on analyzing your dreams.

According to ancient Hindu philosophy and yoga teachings, subtle psychic sense organs in the body channel psychic energies and vital forces related to the glandular and nervous systems. They are also said to link physical, psychic, and superphysical states of consciousness. These centers are called chakras, a Sanskrit term meaning wheels or disks.[1]

According to yoga and Hindu teachings:

Subtle energy flows up the spine following the Chakras. In your body's energy matrix are centers called meridians or nadis. There are 144 Chakras, seven major Chakras, and 12 major

---

[1] The Chakras by C.W. Leadbeater

meridians with 72,000 nadis. Think of these as energy points in your body.

Meditating and doing other work like yoga or exercise can clear the nadis and energy flows. These energy points are related to pressure points on the body. Chinese medicine uses acupuncture to release these energy blockages. Massage therapy and other therapies use pressure points to release the energy blockages. There are many spiritual healing modalities that, in essence, all do the same thing, remove the energy blocks.

In the following text, I will go through the seven Chakras in an abbreviated form for easy reference later when you are analyzing your dreams.

7 Chakra	Colors of the spectrum "Roy G Biv"
1. Root	Red
2. Spleen	Orange
3. Naval	Yellow

4. Heart	Green
5. Throat	Blue
6. Brow	Indigo
7. Crown	Violet

First - Root or Basic Chakra (Muladhara)

- Located At the base of the spine
- It has four sections or petals
- Planet Moon
- Receive into the body two forces that come in at the physical level
- Serpent fire from the earth
- Vitality from the sun
- Astral Centers (awakened functions)
- Home of the Serpent Fire
- Primary Color - Red
- Alternating Red and Orange in hue
- Located at the base of the spine at the 4th Sacral Vertebra
- Safety
- Sexuality
- Security
- Primal needs
- **Blockages**
  - Do not feel safe
  - Worry too much

Chapter 5 Chakras

- Fear
- Paranoia
- Anger

Second - Spleen or Splenic Chakra (*)

- Located Over the spleen
- It has six sections or petals
- Planet Mercury
- Receive into the body two forces that come into it at that physical level
- Serpent fire from the earth
- Vitality from the sun
- Astral Centers (awakened functions)
- Vitalizing the whole astral body
- Enabling the person to travel consciously
- Primary Color – Orange
- Different colors, like glowing sunlight
- Alternating colors of the vital force - red, orange, yellow, green, blue, and violet
- Located over the spleen at the 1st Lumbar Vertebra (Naval area)
- Issues about self
- **Blockages**
    - Lack of self-worth
    - Low Self Esteem

- Worried about how you look
- Worried about how you talk

Third - Naval or Umbilical Chakra (Manipura)

An important Chakra, the third, is primarily being worked on for mastery on the planet. Our spiritual goal is to explore and activate the Fourth Chakra, the heart. We are learning to transition from the third Chakra's wants and desires to the fourth Chakra's attributes.

- Located at the naval, over the solar plexus
- Ten sections
- Planet Venus
- Feelings of emotions of various kinds
- Forces that reach us through our personality
    - Feelings of emotions of various kinds
    - From the lower astral
- Astral Centers (awakened functions)
    - Power
- Primary Color – Yellow
    - Red and green petals

- Located over the navel at the 8th Thoracic Vertebra
- Emotions on the side of hate
  - Scorn
  - Fear
  - Desire to injury
  - Combativeness
  - Disrespect
  - Violence
  - Aggressiveness
  - Jealousy
  - Insolence
- Characterized by
  - Antipathy
  - Self-aggrandizement
  - Desire to take
- Hatred drives one apart from one another
- Yellow
  - Solar Plexus
  - Issues with others
  - Power
- **Blockages**
  - Letting others take advantage of you

- Power over others
- Control Freak

Fourth - Heart or Cardiac Chakra (Anahata)

- Over the heart
- 12 sections
    - Four quadrants, each with three sections
- Planet Sun
- Forces that reach us through our personality
    - From the higher astral plane
- Primary Color - Green
    - Glowing Golden color
- Astral Centers (awakened functions)
    - Power to comprehend
    - Sympathies with the vibrations of other astral entities
    - Expressions of Love
- Located over the heart at the 8th Cervical Vertebra
- Emotions on the side of love
    - Benevolence
    - Helpful
    - Reverence

  - Tenderness
  - Trustfulness
  - Consideration
  - Respect
  - Desire to please
  - Quick insight
- Heart Virtues (wing makers)
  - appreciation
  - compassion
  - forgiveness
  - humility
  - understanding
  - valor
- Characterized by
  - Sympathy
  - Self-sacrifice
  - Desire to give
- Seen as belonging to the spirit
- **Blockages**
  - inability to forgive others
  - Inability to move on from past experiences
  - detaches you from your emotions

- numbing you from love and compassion

Fifth - Throat or Laryngeal Chakra (Vishuddha)

- At the front of the throat
- 16 sections
- Planet Mars
- Forces that reach us through our personality
    - From the lower mind
- Astral Centers (awakened functions)
    - Hearing on the astral plane
- Primary Color - Blue
    - Alternating Blue and Green
- Located at the throat at the 3rd Cervical Vertebra
- Expression
- Communication
- **Blockages**
    - issues with creativity and communication
    - thyroid imbalance
    - sore throat
    - hearing difficulties

Sixth - Brow or Frontal Chakra (Ajna)

- In the space between the eyebrows
- 96 sections
- Planet Jupiter
- Pituitary Gland / Pineal Gland[2]
  - Get activated when a certain amount of spiritual development takes place
- Primary Color - Indigo
  - Divided in half between a Rose - Yellow color and a Purplish-blue color
  - Located on the brow at the 1st Cervical Vertebra
- Astral Centers (awakened functions)
  - Astral Sight
  - Third eye
- Clarity
- Concentration

[2] The litriture is somewhat devided on which gland the Brow Chakra is associated with. Traditionaly it is the Pineal Gland.

- Imagination
- Intuition
- Spiritual perception
- Universal connections
- **Blockages**
  - lose your connection with your inner wisdom
  - feel lost or adrift
  - Imbalance with brain and eyes
  - feel stuck in the day-to-day
  - Headaches, hormone imbalances, nightmares, indecision, burnout, and lack of purpose

Seventh - Crown or Coronal Chakra (Sahasrara)

- Located on the top of the head
- 972 sections
- Planet Saturn
- Pineal Gland / Pituitary Gland
    - Get activated when a certain amount of spiritual development takes place
- Primary Color - Violet
- Located at the crown of the head connected to the Pineal gland
- Astral Centers (awakened functions)
    - Astral life
    - A direct link between physical and higher planes
- **Blockages**
    - Unwillingness to be open to other ideas, thoughts, or knowledge
    - Psychosis
    - Dissociation from the body
    - Being disconnected and ungrounded

Abraham Maslow

Abraham Maslow (1908 – 1970) was an American psychologist best known for creating "Maslow's hierarchy of needs."

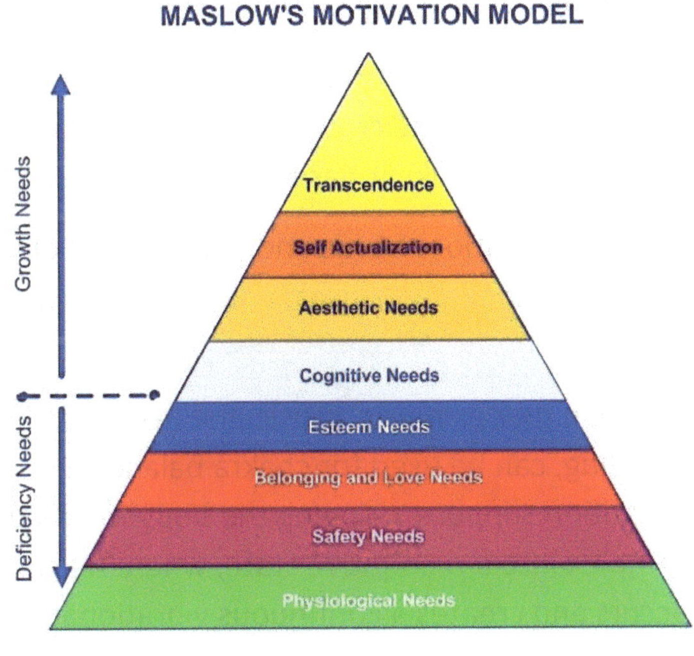

[3]

I find it interesting how Maslow's hierarchy of needs corresponds to the Chakras.

[3] From Wikipedia.org

Sounds

Each Chakra vibrates at different frequencies, from the root to the crown. Each Chakra has its own sound, just like it has its own color.

Sound is vibration. Music and sound, good or bad, influence us and impact our energy systems.

Sound, either as music, musical notes, or chanting, can be used for chakra balancing – repetition supports bringing the body-mind-soul complex into a meditative state, where healing occurs and creates a continuous vibrational environment.

Visualizing the associated chakra color while using sound can deepen and amplify the experience.

The depth and pitch increase with each chakra note or mantra sound, with the deepest sound and lowest pitch at the root, the highest at the crown, and the intermediate chakras calibrated between them. Notes start at middle C.

Bija is the Sanskrit word for the sound essence of the Chakra (its seed).

While meditating, focus your attention on the Chakra as you make its sound, either as a note, vowel, or mantra sound. A vowel or mantra sound can be repeated or chanted three or more times in a row.

Sounds may be soft and gentle - they do not have to be loud. You do not have to be able to carry a tune or sing to sound the chakra notes. You can sound them silently or aloud.

Each chakra sound can be chanted as part of a sound meditation Chakra balancing exercise. Chant the sound for 1 to 5 minutes each, starting at the Root Chakra. Focus on the Chakra as you sound the associated note. To enhance the meditation, visualize the associated Chakra color.

5	4	3	2	1	
Throat	Heart	SolarPle	Sacral	Root	**Chakra**
Blue	Green	Yellow	Orange	Red	**Color**
G	F	E	D	C	**Note / Tone**
EYE / I	AH / A	OH / AH	OOO / O	UH / U	**Vowel**
“ I”	“ father	“ go”	“ you”	“ huh	**Vowel sound**
HAM	YAM	RAM	VAM	LAM	**Mantra (Bija)**
Hum	Yum /	Rum	Vum	Lum	**chakra seed**
Hang	Yang	Rang	Vang	Lang	**syllable**

6	Third -	Indigo	A	AYE / E	" say"	AUM	Aum / ... Aum
7	Crown	Violet	B	EEE / E	" me"	AH	Ahh... / .

Awakening

According to Masonic Lore, Chakras awaken in 3 stages or degrees. Once the 3 stages happen, there is the 33rd degree (the number of vertebras in the spine).

The first degree is the feminine, facilitating control of passion and emotions.

The second degree is the masculine, which facilitates mind control.

The third degree is central energy. When aroused (Sushumna), you are influenced by pure spirit. This awakening allows us to retain full consciousness on higher plains and bring a clear memory of the experience back into the physical brain.

The stick of Brahma, two snakes spiraling up the staff, is the spine. The energy, called the Kundalini or serpent fire, travels up along the two channels (the two snakes). The wings at the top of the staff are the caduceus of Mercury, showing conscious flight through higher planes of existence.

[4]

This symbol is also known as the medical symbol. A staff or rod with a snake curled around it. The Rod of Aesculapius (also called Asklepios) is the ancient mythical god of

---

[4] https://www.medicinenet.com/medical_symbol/definition.htm

medicine. Asklepios may have been a real person renowned for his gentle remedies and humane treatment of the mentally ill.

Chapter 6 Pineal Gland

"Decalcify the pineal gland with the detergent of imagination."

— Dean Cavanagh

Chapter 6 Pineal Gland

Called the 3rd eye, the Pineal Gland is part of the photo-neuro-endocrine system, composed of the retina, central nervous system, and pineal gland. The pineal gland is a pea-sized gland situated on the sagittal line in the exact geometric center of the brain. It is solid, pine-cone shaped, red-grey color, approximately 5–9 mm long and 1–5 mm wide, and weighs 100–180 mg. Rather than the rods and cones, it is a newly discovered subgroup of photosensitive retinal ganglion cells.[5] The pineal gland even has vitreous fluid inside. This sensor is wired into the visual cortex in the brain.

"***The photoreceptors of the retina strongly resemble the cells of the pineal gland***." Dr. David Klein, Science Daily.

The pineal gland is a *photo-neuro-endocrine organ* that secretes Serotonin, Melatonin, and N,N-Dimethyltryptamine.

---

[5] Pfeffer M, Korf HW, Wicht H. Synchronizing effects of melatonin on diurnal and circadian rhythms. Gen Comp Endocrinol. 2018;258:215–221

Chapter 6 Pineal Gland

"***seat of the soul***" -- René Descartes (1596–1650)

Floride causes The pineal gland to calcify. This calcification will show up on X-rays, marking the brain's center. Calcification is often used to identify brain problems when off-center.

"The light of the body is the eye: if therefore thine eye be single, thy whole body shall be full of light."

-- Jesus in Matthew 6-22

During out-of-body experiences, people report seeing a silver cord linking their astral body back to their physical body located between the eyes or at the back of the head where the pineal gland is.

Rhythms

Our bodies are affected by various natural rhythms throughout the day. These rhythms cause our bodies to produce and secrete chemicals to regulate bodily functions.

- **Ultradian rhythm** is a recurrent cycle repeated throughout a 24-hour day.
- **Circadian rhythms** complete one cycle daily,

Circadian rhythms found in plants, animals, fungi, and even bacteria use external signals, such as light, to trigger the cyclical release of chemicals. This release of chemicals signals the body when to start and stop different actions. Circadian rhythms govern activities such as bee feeding times, plant leaf movement, and fungi DNA replication. In humans, circadian rhythms are best known for controlling our sleep schedules. The Circadian rhythms, along with light sensitivity, control the production of Melatonin.

Melatonin

Melatonin helps to maintain our 24-hour sleep schedule. Our bodies translate information about the time of day into melatonin production. This process starts in the eye's retina. When the retina is exposed to light, photoreceptor cells send a signal relayed from the retina to an area of the brain called the suprachiasmatic nucleus. The suprachiasmatic nucleus stimulates the production of Melatonin. The result is that we feel sleepy. Photoreceptor cells In the retina turn on or off Melatonin production. Melatonin is produced mainly by the pineal gland and is made in small amounts in the retina, lens, iris, ciliary body, lacrimal gland, skin, and gut. Blue light of a specific frequency triggers this on-and-off switch for Melatonin production.

It is important to note that many of the LED light bulbs in use today emit this blue light and interfere with Melatonin production and, thus, our sleep cycles. That is why your computer and smartphones have a night and day mode for the screen. The night mode filters the harmful blue light. There is also some indication that this blue light accelerates macular degeneration. You can buy special blue blocker glasses. My eyeglass lenses are specifically designed to filter out that frequency of light.

The synthesis of Melatonin occurs in four steps.

1. Tryptophan is converted into 5-Hydroxytryptophan
2. 5-Hydroxytryptophan is converted to Serotonin
3. Serotonin is converted into N-Acetylserotonin
4. N-Acetylserotonin is converted into Melatonin

Serotonin N-Acetyltransferase (SNAT) is an enzyme that adds an acetyl group to Serotonin to produce N-Acetylserotonin, which peaks when it is dark outside.

In short, this means that when the blue light is absent, your body says it's time to go to bed and starts producing Melatonin.

The neurotransmitter acetylcholine is at its strongest both during REM (rapid eye movement) sleep and while you are awake. Acetylcholine triples during REM sleep and seems to help your brain keep information-gathering mode while awake and sleeping. The neurotransmitter dopamine may trigger sleep disorders such as restless legs syndrome.

Caffeine and Melatonin

The Caffeine molecule and the Melatonin molecule are very similar. Caffeine and Melatonin bind to the same receptors. Melatonin cannot bind to the receptor if too much caffeine is present. Sleep becomes difficult. It is not until the caffeine releases, allowing the Melatonin to connect, that we start to get sleepy.

Things to help you sleep

Magnesium and Melatonin supplements help sleep. Please consult your health professional before taking supplements.

Lavender oil (aroma) helps to reduce anxiety and depression, and it also makes you sleepy.

Get more light during the day and less at night.

Turn off all blue lights two hours before bedtime, or wear blue blocker glasses.

Cooler temperatures while sleeping.

Exercise also helps with better sleep quality.

Fermented Skat Live Oil from Green Pasture is supposed to decalcify the pineal gland. Green Pastures (www.greenpasture.org) has come under scrutiny over the past few years, so investigate before buying. Skate liver oil is also supposed to have health benefits for your teeth.

Melatonin Effects

Melatonin has many beneficial effects on the body. Melatonin production may decrease as we age and with today's lifestyle. Supplements may be helpful. Below are some of the benefits of Melatonin in the body

- Sexual organs
- Downregulation of thyroid activity

- hypothermic
- Sleep inducing
- Hypotensive by increasing norepinephrine levels
- Regulating cardiac beta receptors
- Increasing mesenteric arterial dilation capacity
- Immunoregulatory
- Antioxidant
- clearing free radicals
- Thymic modulator
- Oncostatic – helps to halt the spread of cancer
- Neuroprotector - recovery or regeneration of the nervous system

Melatonin Receptors

Melatonin receptors are present in various locations in the body:

- The cerebral cortex - the cerebrum's outer layer, is composed of folded gray matter and plays a vital role in consciousness.

- Hippocampus - brain structure embedded deep into the temporal lobe having a major role in learning and memory.
- Basal nuclei - a group of subcortical structures found deep within the white matter of the brain. They form a part of the extrapyramidal motor system and work in tandem with the pyramidal and limbic systems.
- Diencephalon - found just above the brainstem between the cerebral hemispheres
- Mesencephalon - the forward-most portion of the brainstem, is associated with vision, hearing, motor control, sleep and wakefulness, arousal (alertness), and temperature regulation.[6]
- Retina - a layer of tissue in the back of your eye that senses light and sends images to your brain

---

[6] Breedlove, Watson, & Rosenzweig. Biological Psychology, 6th Edition, 2010, pp. 45-46

- Choroidal layer - a thin, pigmented vascular network consisting of three layers (from inner to outer): choriocapillaris, stroma, and lamina fusca. The choriocapillaris provide nutrients to the RPE and the outer third of the retina.[7]
- Sclera - The white outer coating of the eye.
- Cornea – The eye's clear, protective outer layer.
- Ciliary body - The part of the eye that connects the iris to the choroid.

Melatonin is seen to have a regenerative effect on corneal lesions and the regulation of intraocular pressure. Many believe it may act as an antiglaucoma agent, slowing the onset of glaucoma.

Melatonin may also have a protective effect against X-ray radiation.

---

[7] Caroline J. Zeiss, ... Piper M. Treuting, in Comparative Anatomy and Histology (Second Edition), 2018

DMT - N,N-Dymethyltriptamine

Produced by the Pineal Gland, DMT is often called the God Molecule for its stimulating effect on the Pineal Gland to have spiritual encounters when DMT levels are increased. DMT falls into the hallucinogen category.

DMT is found in many plants, stimulating the pineal gland and promoting a spiritual experience. Ayahuasca is a ceremonial brew used for centuries for physical, mental, and spiritual well-being. Used in many shamanistic ceremonies, DMT in Ayahuasca directly affects the pineal gland. Participants often report having spiritual insight and receiving profound messages during the ceremonies.

By becoming adept at meditation and paying attention to our dreams we can accomplish the same results as in Ayahuasca ceremonies, receiving messages and insights from our higher consciousness and spirit guides.

When the Pineal gland opens up, dreaming becomes very important for polarization. You can call on spirit to guide you. Feeling pressure inside or the top of your head or a tingling sensation between your eyes during meditation is your Pineal Gland being activated. It is theorized that the Pinela Gland generates a field around it that enters another dimension, the spiritual dimension. It is thought that the Pineal Gland field can be expanded to encompass your head area or larger, creating a portal through which to travel. This is also believed to be why we see angels and saints with a yellow halo around their heads.

According to secret projects in the government reported by whistleblowers, the Sumarieans reverse-engineered the Pineal Gland and created a device, the secret projects called Project Looking Glass. Looking Glass is supposed to allow a person to walk up to it and think about what they wish to see, and then they will see possible future results from their thoughts. For example, what happens if I do "xxx"? What will the result of that action be?

Chapter 6 Pineal Gland

The Pineal Gland is thought to capture minute sparks, which translate into images and sound and are transferred to the visual cortex in the brain, allowing us to see future events or other such things. You can find more information on Project Looking Glass by searching the web.

Pineal Gland Representations

References to the Pineal Gland appear worldwide in various forms: the Sumerian, Greek, and Roman cultures. Even on the Pope's staff, the Vatican's "Court of the Pine Cone" refers to the Pineal Gland. It is depicted as a pine cone either alone or as a headdressing.

Chapter 7 Lucid Dreaming

"Don't let your dreams end in your sleep. Bring them over here!"

— Michael Bassey Johnson, The Oneironaut's Diary

Chapter 7 Lucid Dreaming

Lucid dreaming is being aware you are dreaming while you are dreaming. When you become aware you are dreaming, you can take control of the dream and change its outcome. Controlling the dream will cause changes in your mind that will help you overcome the dream's theme. You can do many things when you become aware you are in a dream. You can Fly and visit other places. You can change the outcome. For example, if you feel stuck in a room, you can create a new door and walk through it to another part of the dream. You can heal yourself or others in the dream. Most importantly, you can remember more details of the dream. I knew of one person who would freeze-frame the dream and then take measurements of the angle of the sun and other items in the dream to figure out the time of day based on the sun's angles.

I had a dream one time that was so vivid it was as if I was awake. I heard a noise and wondered where the source was. The only difference was that the room was very bright, the light coming from all over, not just the light bulbs. Looking back, it seemed more real than usual. I looked all over the room, looking for the noise. I looked out the window, and it, too, looked normal. Then I realized I was dreaming. Then, the dream dissolved. It was a fascinating experience. The goal is to have every dream become as lucid as that one.

Sometimes, I am lucid, but the dream seems dull, not as bright, and with not as much detail. I can change the dream in some lucid dreams and control what happens. Other times, I am just aware I am in a dream and watch it like watching a movie, with vivid details and recall.

Validate your reality

Validate your reality to learn to become lucid in your dreams. By creating the habit of validating your reality, you will, by habit, validate your reality in the dream and then become aware you are dreaming.

You should test or validate your reality at least 20 times per day. Making validating your reality a habit makes it easier to realize you are in a dream and become lucid. Once you realize you are in a dream, all you need to do is say, "This is a dream." Once you know you are in a dream, you can take charge and control the dream.

There are many ways to validate your reality.

Object Permanence

To test for object permanence, look at a point and study it. Look away for a few seconds. Then, look back and see if anything has changed in the scene. In a dream, things will often look different when you look back.

Reading

Reading is often tricky in a dream. It frequently seems like the words change as you read them, and it is frustrating to try to read them.

Impossible Things

Does something look like it does not belong? For example, a car with no wheels that you can drive. Animals are talking to you. Anything that would not happen in the waking world should make you aware you are in a dream.

Other Tests

Mirrors. Does your reflection seem normal?

Solid objects. While pushing your hand against a wall or table, it may go through. Some people push their fingers into their opposite palms. Push on a wall; does it move or seem flexible?

Hands. Look at your hands. Do they look normal? Pull one finger and see if it stretches.

Time. While dreaming, the time on a clock seems to change constantly. Time will barely change while you are awake.

Breathing. A popular reality check involves pinching your nose and seeing if you can breathe. If you can still breathe, you're dreaming. Breathing underwater is another sign.

Secure the Dream

To dream consistently, get enough sleep. Seven to 9 hours a night is recommended. Keep regular sleep schedules. Stay hydrated. Drink two eight-ounce glasses of water when you get up in the morning. Remove caffeine, or at least reduce caffeine as the day progresses. Eat a proper diet. Get exercise. Stretch before going to bed. Go to bed and get up at the same time every day.

Dreamsigns

Identify a "dreamsign," something irregular or strange in the dream. An example is the ability to fly.

Look for dream signs

- Flying
- Irrational thinking
- Weak or strong emotions toward the situation
- Meeting deceased people
- Meeting Celebrities

Other Devices

There are devices to help you identify that you are dreaming. One such device is a mask with blinking lights. The mask recognizes that you are in REM sleep by eye movement and then flashes lights. You will see these lights in your dream, which is supposed to alert you that you are in REM sleep and become lucid. I have not used these devices and do not know of anyone who has. If you decide to try one, do your research first.

Chapter 7 Lucid Dreaming

Chapter 8 What interferes with dreaming?

"Dreams are divine gems. Find and keep them safe."

— Michael Bassey Johnson, The Oneironaut's Diary

Chapter 8 What interferes with dreaming?

Many things interfere with dreaming: Daily stress, work stress, family stress, worrying, smoking, spicy foods, and social pressures affect dreaming. They interfere with REM sleep. Certain antidepressants seem to suppress the REM state and interfere with dreaming. Not enough sleep, too much sleep, alcohol, and cannabis also affect the dream state.

Wi-Fi and Cell phone singles too close to you while you sleep affect sleep. Remove Wi-Fi access points from your bedroom. Keep cell phones and other devices at least 6 feet from you while you sleep to reduce radio frequency interference.

Chapter 9 How to Remember Your Dreams

"Dreams are illustrations...from the book your soul is writing about you."

-- Marsha Norman

Chapter 9 How to Remember Your Dreams

Many people say I don't dream. Everybody dreams. If you did not dream, you would go crazy in a few days. Your brain and mind need to go to Alpha periodically. If you do not, you will show signs of going crazy. You may not remember your dreams often, but you can change that.

Before you go to sleep, meditate and tell yourself that you want to remember a dream and that you will remember a dream. You may wake up after your dream, and you may be groggy. You will need to write it down. When you wake up, read your dream notes and write down any additional notes in the morning.

You can program yourself by saying: "I want to remember my dreams, and I will remember my dreams, AND THIS IS SO." Record your dream on paper or in a recorder, as mentioned in a previous chapter, when you wake up after having dreams. Remembering your dreams after waking up is challenging if you do not record them. The "AND THIS IS SO" tells your mind this is how it is, no debate about it. Say it with emphasis.

It's not just "I want to remember my dreams," be specific:

- Where was I?
- Who was I talking to?
- Where was I going?
- What was I doing?
- What were the symbols in the dream?

In the book *Lucid Dreaming* by Stephen LaBerge, Ph. D., he suggests many techniques to induce lucid dreaming.

Set up dream recall by setting the intention to remember your dreams. When you go to bed and before you fall asleep, repeat mentally many times:

- Next time I dream, I will remember I'm dreaming
- Next time I dream, I will remember to recognize that I'm dreaming

- The next time I dream, I recognize I'm dreaming and do whatever I want to do in that lucid dream.
- When "such–and–such" happens, I will remember to do "so-and-so."

Then, see yourself becoming lucid in your dreams, repeating these lines until you set your intention.

When you wake in the middle of the night or the morning, think about returning to the dream and then do the following:

- Do not move your position upon awakening.
- Identify the dreamsigns.
- Acknowledge that the dreamsigns only happen when you dream.
- Scan for clues to what you were dreaming.
- Validate the dream.
- Feel the excitement.
- Replay the dream with validation.
- Have childlike excitement for the dream.

- What was my mood in the dream?
- What feelings did I have?
- Did I catch any fragments or images?
- What were my thoughts?
- Why was I thinking that?

Dreamscape

The Dreamscape is my term for the dream landscape. You can talk to your Dreamscape when you are in a lucid dream. Ask your dream questions, and the dream will respond to you. I'm unsure who answers, but when I ask or shout to the Dreamscape, "What does ... mean?" I always get an answer. I often ask my spirit guides questions about my dream and its symbols to understand it better. In one of my classes, we introduce guides to ask questions and receive information. Talking to my guides has proven helpful in understanding my dreams.

In my Dream Secrets Class, I do conditioning exercises that help to trigger lucid dreaming. One method I condition is the "two-finger" technique. I take you through a meditation where I condition that placing your index and middle finger, the two-finger technique, in the middle of your forehead between your eyes will trigger easier dream recall and induce lucid dreaming.

Chapter 10 Your Lucid – Now What

"The best-laid plans of mice and men often go awry."

-- Robert Burns

Chapter 10 Your Lucid – Now What

You've become lucid in your dream. Now what. It's time to build a plan for what you will do in the dream when you become lucid.

Build a plan. Spend time thinking about how to attack the dream when you become lucid.

Decide what you want to accomplish. Here are some ideas:

- Go around the dream and ask questions
- Shout out to the dream. What does this mean? "This" refers to something in the dream.
- Leave the dream area and fly around your neighborhood.
- Look for other people having dreams and meet them.
- Talk to the different Characters in the dream
    - The objects
    - The people
    - The authority figures
- Change the dream dynamics to provide a different outcome

- Changing the dream dynamics stimulates your mind with alternative solutions to the theme of the dream, a very effective way to use your dream time.

While awake, thinking and formulating a dream plan will let you maximize your dream. I became aware of this in one dream where I was looking at a picture. The images kept changing in the picture. I realized I was in a dream and said, "This is a dream." Then I thought, "Now, what do I do?" I did not want to fly away from the dream. As I thought about what I wanted to do, the dream dissolved.

It's always a good idea to be prepared for what comes next. Formulating a plan before becoming lucid will maximize your dream experience. Remember, you do not have to follow your plan. You can change what you decide to do while in the dream. Having a plan will get you started to do something.

Chapter 10 Your Lucid – Now What

Chapter 11 Keeping a Log

"You must learn to control your dreams or your dreams will forever control you."

-- Wayne Gerard Trotman

Chapter 11 Keeping a Log

Now, it is time to create a dream journal. There are several ways to start to journal your dream.

The easiest is to keep a book by your bed to write down the dream when you wake up. The problems you run into with this method are that your writing is illegible or sentences are written on top of one another.

I once had a dream where I woke up in the middle of the night and wrote about four pages of very detailed notes on the dream. When I woke, I was eager to read and review my dream, only to find out that I had four illegible scribbled pages. When I program myself to journal my dreams, I add, "I will write them down legibly."

Using a recorder can simplify things. A recorder works well if you can speak clearly and will not wake anyone sleeping next to you. The issue with this method is that you must listen to the recording and transcribe the dream into your dream journal. You can also use your phone as they have recorder apps. Be sure you can operate the recorder in the dark with your eyes closed. It is frustrating to take the time to record or journal your dream only to find out the entry is not usable.

Another way of recording your dreams is to use your computer. Leave a laptop near your bed. Set a word processor program to be ready so that it is ready for you to start typing when you open up your computer. The less you have to open your eyes, the better. The less you need to focus your vision, the easier it is to stay in the semi-dream state, achieving better dream recall. I timestamp all journal entries for other journals I keep. In Microsoft Word, pressing Alt-Shift-T will insert the date and time, although I have not used this method to record my dreams.

I recommend that you start to keep a dream log. To keep a dream log, you need to:

- Remember your dreams
- Record your dreams
- Analyze or interpret your dreams

Chapter 11 Keeping a Log

To analyze your dreams, take a page in a notebook or use a word processor to record your dreams. I use the left page to journal daily activities, dates and times, events of the day, feelings, food, and the right page for the details of dreams.

Record the date and time of the dream and the details of the dream. I recently added feelings to the log. Adding feelings was inspired when I talked to a friend's son who was home from a tour in Iraq and has been suffering from post-traumatic stress. Another friend, a Vietnam-era veteran, said he keeps that in his dream log, which has helped him overcome some war issues. He noted that some American Indian guides also recommended it to him. You may want to record food and see how it affects your dreams and life. There is growing evidence that as you improve your diet, your thoughts change from toxic thoughts to good ones.

Then, after a few days or a few weeks, go back and review your dream log. You may notice that, for example, if you have a dream about ice (which is one of my symbols), there is something that you "should" watch on TV the next day. As you build your dream log, you will notice and connect events in the dream and things in your daily life. Messages from your spirit guides, subconscious, higher self, and many other sources fill your dreams.

Pay attention to the little things in the dream. Something that looks insignificant in the dream, for example, the number of items in the dream, may be the point of the dream.

When you get adept at remembering your dreams, you can start to control your dreams. Controlling your dreams is when you are aware you are dreaming in the dream; this is called "Lucid dreaming." You may stop the dream and do something like take out a tape measure and measure things. Stop the dream and investigate where a door goes. Put a door in your dream where one does not exist and go through it, fly, go to other planets, etc. It becomes an adventure. As time goes on, dreams can be as vivid as when you are awake. I have had a few of these, not as much as I would like, but it was very confusing the first couple of times I had a vivid dream. I thought I was awake and was walking around the room. A few things were odd, like the color of the light, etc. A few times, I realized I was in a dream and started to control them and go in a different direction than the dream was going in. Controlling your dreams like this is a lot of fun.

I tend to get a lot of numbers in my dreams. For example, I had a series of dreams where I counted things in the scene. In one case, it was the number of people in the car with me. The number is related to numerology, which gave it a specific meaning that I was able to use and understand.

Chapter 12 Segmented Sleep

"For a dreamer is one who can only find his way by moonlight, and his punishment is that he sees the dawn before the rest of the world."

-- Oscar Wilde

Chapter 12 Segmented Sleep

You can use segmented sleep if you wake in the middle of the night and can't get back to sleep, often after sleeping for four to six hours. You feel wide awake and can't fall back to sleep. Get up for 1 hour, 2 hours max. Do something, read, write, or work on something. Write down any dreams you can remember. Then, go back to sleep for, let's say, three hours.

The benefit of segmented sleep is like getting two nights' sleep in one. Getting up resets your gland system, causing it to restart the process, and you benefit.

Many people will do segmented sleep daily, only in the morning. For example, they awake at seven am, stay up for an hour, and then go back to sleep to enter a lucid dream state. Many have reported success at entering lucid dreaming every morning after they return to sleep.

Chapter 13 Keeping the dream going

Chapter 13 Keeping the dream going

"We are such stuff as dreams are made on, and our little life is rounded with a sleep."

-- William Shakespeare

Chapter 13 Keeping the dream going

When you first start to lucid dream, the excitement of realizing you are in a dream can cause it to dissolve. To keep the dream going, begin to listen to your Dream Voice. Remain calm in the dream. You can stabilize your dream by saying, "Now I am Dreaming."

If the dream shows signs of ending, in the book *Lucid Dreaming* by Stephen LaBerge, Ph. D., he suggests spinning yourself in the dream and saying, "The next thing I see will be a dream."

David Wilcock suggests shooting your hands out and shouting in the dream: "CLARITY NOW!"

Also, avoid thinking about your body or moving, as this will aid in dissolving the dream.

Talking to characters in the dream will sometimes keep the dream going. Ask the characters who they are and what they represent. Or shout those questions out to the Dreamscape.

Chapter 14 What does the dream mean?

"Your vision will become clear when you look into your heart."

-- Carl Jung

Chapter 14 What does the dream mean?

The Law of One by Elkins, Rueckaert, and McCary, a channeled book, has this to say about dreams:

- Ra 86.12 – Dream activity is a finely wrought and excellently fashioned bridge from conscious to unconscious.[8]
- Lack of dreaming can cause seriously distorted people

Dream Voice

I heard this from David Wilcocks, but I have also encountered it in other works. Listen to your dream voice and record anything you hear when you wake up and are still in a dreamy state. The idea is to record everything from this faint voice and DO NOT INTERPRET anything. Do not change what is being gifted to you by your interpretation. You want to record what you hear and not pay attention to what you hear.

---

[8] The Law of One Search Results for 'finely wrought'. https://www.lawofone.info/results.php?q=finely+wrought&st=all&m=0

Chapter 14 What does the dream mean?

Later, you can interpret and look for understanding when you review the recording.

I often wake up after a dream and review the contents in detail. What does each character or thing in the dream mean? How does it apply to my life? What lesson can I learn, or what message is the dream telling me? Sometimes, I meditate on the symbols for days before I realize the answer.

I often ask for clarification from my spirit guides about my dreams in my daily meditations.

Chapter 14 What does the dream mean?

Chapter 15 Analyze the Dream

"Dream lofty dreams, and as you dream, so shall you become. Your vision is the promise of what you shall one day be; your ideal is the prophecy of what you shall at last unveil."

– James Allen

Chapter 15 Analyze the Dream

There are many techniques for learning and discovering your dream symbols. There are many books on the subject. At first, symbols may be somewhat universal, but as you become more adept at dreaming and recalling your dreams, your symbols become tailored to you. One technique I read in a book, but I'm not sure which one, is to yell out or speak out in the dream, assuming you are lucid. What does ... mean? The ... is whatever the symbol in the dream is.

I dreamed the scene was like Paul Revere during the Revolutionary War a while ago. Remember, Paul was the guy who said: "One if by land, two if by sea." I was on a horse and galloped down the road. Wondering what the horse represented, I asked, and a voice said, "It is you charting a new path in your life."

It made sense after I thought about it for a while. Another way to do this is when you fall asleep. I sometimes enter a semi-dream state, dreaming and awake, not a Lucid dream, but halfway there. I review certain symbols and ask what they mean. Sometimes, I get answers to what they mean. Sometimes, no answer comes.

Whatever happens, it is exciting to experience and learn what these symbols mean. As you learn what symbols mean, it becomes easier to interpret what new symbols mean and understand the language of the dream.

Pay attention to details, small things in the dream, colors, geometric shapes, and the color of your shirt or clothes. These details often hold more information and symbols than the main context of the dream. These tiny symbols may be an essential part of the dream.

Nightmares

What are nightmares? Nightmares can mean you are not paying attention to your dreams. For example, if we were in a movie theater and you were in front of me talking during the movie. If I politely ask you to stop talking and you ignore me. Then I ask you a little louder, and I feel ignored, then I scream at you to shut up during the movie. I will most likely get your attention. Nightmares can be the same thing. They will stop if you start to record your dreams and look for meaning.

Confronting Fears in your mind

Suppose you confront scary things like a monster in meditation or a dream. One technique is to point your finger at it to make them smaller. Every time you point your finger at them, they get smaller and smaller. At some point, you can pick up the monster, fit it in your hand, and play with it. Changing the scary thing will make it less scary and give you control over the issue. You can then analyze it, figure out what it represents, and change the situation or monster into something positive.

In one of my classes, a child was doing a guided meditation and said, "I'm scared." When asked why, they said, "There is a scary monster in front of me." We told them to point their finger at it, and each time they did, the monster would get smaller and smaller. Then, a few minutes later, they were laughing. When asked, "What are you laughing at?" They said, "I am playing with the monster in my hand." The monster went from a scary thing to a plaything. A technique they can use for the rest of their lives when confronted with issues like this.

I was reviewing the idea of confronting your monster. A student said they often have the same scary dream. I suggested that they face the monster. The next day, they said they had the dream again; this time, they turned and faced the monster. It went from several monsters to one and then turned into her father. She then conversed with him and cleared up whatever the issue was. The nightmare stopped. The dream was trying to tell her something needed attention—another reason to record your dreams.

Symbols

Everything in the dream is an aspect of you. Each symbol, person, or event represents something about you in the current dream context. When you analyze the dream, you must look at each item and ask how this relates to you. What does that symbol, person, or event mean to you? What does it represent? When a character, either person or object, appears, ask yourself. When did I know this symbol? For example, you are driving a car. The car was your first car, and you had it between the ages of 17 and 21. What did that car represent to you at that time? What the car meant to you at that time conveys its meaning in the dream. The same goes for people, events, or anything that may have happened during a specific period in your life. Compare that meaning to your current situation.

Authority figures, like police, fire, security guards, people of other races, or aliens, could be higher being helping you. When he first controlled his dreams, a person I know would freeze-frame the dream. While the dream was frozen, he noticed a person standing on the side of the dream, with his arms folded, observing what he was doing. He was not frozen but seemed to be watching. That person later showed up as one of his spirit guides. In one of my other classes, I teach students to go to, what we call, their laboratory level. We create a specific place in our mind to do work at the laboratory level. The work is healing, self-programming, or investigation. In the laboratory, we introduce counselors or spirit guides to assist you in answering questions and any other help you need.

Animals typically can be aspects of your lower primal self or lower Chakras. But they do not have to be. As I mentioned earlier, I dreamt of a horse showing up. Later, when I discussed this dream with a friend, he noted that the horse could have represented my move to Kentucky. Kentucky is known for horses. I moved about a year after the dream to Kentucky.

The ultimate reason for a dream is that your higher self teaches you lessons, alerts you to things to be aware of, or gives you emotional support. The dream is the most important thing you need to know that day. Dreams often bring your attention to areas of importance.

See your dreams like a treasure chest of value. Remember them with childlike excitement to discover their meaning. Dream messages come through symbols, rarely directly. They teach us love, forgiveness, self-acceptance, patience, and much more. Dreams help us solve problems.

In 1846, Elias Howe Jr. pattened the first sewing machine. Elias was frustrated working on the sewing machine. He slept and dreamed he was working for a tribal chief in a far-off land. The chief gave him 24 hours to get his sewing machine working, or he would be put to death. He gave up in the dream, and the chief's soldiers came to get him carrying spears. Elisa noticed that the spear had eyes on the tip. Elisa had been trying to get his sewing machine working with the eye at the other end like a manual sewing needle. He woke up around 3 am, and by 9 am, he had a working sewing machine.

Not only can dreams provide solutions to problems, but you can also program your dreams to find solutions to your problems.

Interpreting

Upon waking from a dream, note:

- Where was I
    - Indoors or outdoors
- Colors
- How I feel
- What is the emotional resonance of the dream
- Who was I talking to
- Where was I going
- What was I doing
- What were the symbols in the dream
- How did I get there
- What can I do

The Four Elements

Many ancient traditions represent the four elements: water, fire, air, and earth. Each of these elements has universal meanings when they appear in a dream.

- Water
    - Emotions
    - Sadness
    - Grief
    - Sorrow
- Fire
    - Anger
    - Intensity
    - Passion
    - Could represent a big argument
- Air
    - The winds of change
    - Intellect
    - It could be negative or disruptive, destabilizing
    - Intellectual activity
    - Do more meditation and grounding
- Earth
    - Grounding
    - Nurturing

- Renewal
- Go out into nature
- Soil

Dream Landscape or DreamScape

According to deep insider testimony relay by David Wilcock, the "secret" projects defined something they call the "Dream Landscape." I call this and any dream the "Dreamscape." They report that one needs to understand the dream landscape to advance psychically and emotionally. Understanding the dream landscape helps overcome psychic blocks and advance your spiritual development.

The dream landscape is a symbolic representation of your personality matrix and, as a whole, is your personality. As you dream each night, you move around your dream landscape. Every time you return to the same section of your dream landscape, the dream's meaning is the same, but the symbols change. As you start to understand your dreams and heal the aspects the dream is telling you about, you can move to a more extensive area of that portion of the landscape. Opening up new areas to work on and new regions to explore. Every part of the dream landscape is you. The dream landscape is out of time. Out of time means that the lessons are something you need to overcome and heal from to move on in your life. For example, I had recurring dreams in the dream landscape that showed me water in different forms. I would have a dream or two, go for maybe a week, and then have another dream or two with the same representation. The water represented the emotional sadness or grief that I had suppressed. With meditation, it took me a while to understand the cause, but finally, I identified the reason. The sadness and anger were due to decisions I had made earlier in my life that I had repressed. After determining this, I worked on forgiving myself for those decisions and moved on, opening up a new area to explore the next time I visited that portion of the dream landscape.

Heal and move on

Figuring out the blocks and the reasons for the dream can be challenging. We must do this work to heal ourselves and open up new possibilities in our lives and dreams. We need to forgive the trauma we have experienced. This work is not easy, and often, it is tough to look at ourselves this deeply. But we must advance in our lives.

Making a visual representation or drawing of the dream landscape is helpful. Making a map will help you identify areas and speed up your progress. As you expand your dream landscape, new things show up for you to explore.

The distance between objects in your dream landscape indicates the size of your soul—the bigger the area, the bigger the room for symbolism. You must go through the "Dark Night of the Soul" (part of the Hero’s Journey) to move on.

The Hero's Journey

Joseph Campbell describes the Hero's Journey as a theme of this reality and the universe. We see the Hero's journey in many aspects of life in movies and our lives.

In movies, it goes like this:

- The Hero – that's you, starts with some issues.
- You meet a villain (who could be your ideal mate), The opposition you must overcome.
- You meet a sage who guides you on overcoming your liabilities to meet your objective.
- You face some challenge or objection that deflates you and makes you give up. (The dark night of the soul)
- Then you meet your guide again, and they teach you and give you support that you can do it.
- You meet your objectives and live happily ever after

Analysis

Chapter 15 Analyze the Dream

It's time now to analyze your position in the dream landscape. Height in the dream landscape indicates your vibrational level, which relates to your chakra development. Ground-level in your dream is typically the third Chakra. Above the surface are your higher Chakras. Below the surface, represent your lower Chakras issues.

Left or a left turn represents service to self or the negative polarity. Right or a right turn represents service to others or positive polarity. The same is true for the left or right ear ringing in your ears.

Pay attention to these items in your dream:

- Height above the ground
- Which direction are you going
- What elements are present? Air, earth, fire, and water
- How fast are you moving?

Direction or movement in the dream denotes time. Time moves in the direction you are facing. Forward is the future. Backward is the past.

Speed of travel denotes your spiritual growth progress.

- Being stuck in one place indicates you are not learning your lessons.
- Walking, you are progressing at an average pace.
- Running, you're at an accelerated pace.
- Bicycle, even faster pace
- In a car – Rapid spiritual progress
- In a bus or a train – your growing fast with others (it holds multiple people)
- In a Plane or a Spaceship – excellent progress with multiple people
- Levitation or Flying – Profound spiritual improvement

Color is important and relates to your Chakra colors.

1. Red – Safety, sexuality, security
2. Orange – How you see yourself, lack of self-esteem, acceptance

3. Yellow – How you see others, power over them, or them over you
4. Green – Love and service to others. Your heart is open
5. Light Blue – Light, wisdom, honor, communications
6. Indigo – Unity Consciousness, Law of One, Psychic ability
7. Violet – infinit Intelligece

The language of dreams starts out using universal symbols. As you progress, the symbols become more specific to you. In my experience, if you use a guidebook or other dream interpretation references, your symbols will relate to them. I use a number chart I found online by Doreen Virtue called "The Number Sequences From The Angels." I often have numbers in my dreams. I use the chart to determine the meaning of the number sequence.

Symbolic meaning shows up everywhere. In "You Can Heal Your Life" by Louise Hay, she relates problems with different body parts to your issues. Understand your issues, and you can heal those parts of your body that are having trouble.

Repetitive dreams indicate repetitive behavior and lessons you are not learning, such as addictions or stumbling blocks. Your dream always gives you advice. A child in your dream is your inner child. Huge areas are good and show you that you are opening up.

Negative entities in your dreams are sometimes demonic beings. If they are pulling your left arm, for example, or pulling you down into the basement, they are trying to control you and get you off your spiritual development. If this happens, say: **I love you. I reject your service. It is not helpful for me at this time. Thank you and begone.** You can always use the Hawaiian folk law teaching for forgiveness, which is called Ho'oponopono.

"I'M SORRY, PLEASE FORGIVE ME. I LOVE YOU, THANK YOU."

The Ho'oponopono prayer is helpful in many situations, not only in your dreams.

Nightmares, Monsters, and Scary things

Your dream is your dream, and nothing can hurt you. Facing the scary thing in a dream will often cause it to transform into the real issue. A student of mine had a dream. There were snakes in her dream. She had this dream many times, and it was scary. After talking about this, she had the dream again and decided to face her fear. Instead of running, she turned and faced it. The many snakes turned into one. The one snake turned into her father. She then realized the issues the dream was telling her about and resolved her father issues.

Point your finger at the scary thing and say: "every time I point my finger at you, you will get smaller and smaller." Scary dreams are often your subconscious's way of getting your attention. It's as if we were in a movie theater, and the person in front of us is talking. You say, please be quiet, and they ignore you. Then you repeat it, and they ignore you. Then you shout out loud, BE QUIET! And they finally hear you. The dream is trying to get your attention. Paying attention to your dreams will reduce nightmares and scary things in your dreams. Embrace them, forgive them, and face them.

When food shows up in dreams, it often means you need spiritual sustenance.

Understanding the issue and the dream's meaning is not always easy. There are details in every aspect of the dream to help you overcome the problems. Understanding the archetypes is a challenge as most people never fully understand all the archetypes in the dream at a conscious level. Little details in the dream often contain more information than the action taking place.

Chapter 16 Archetypes

"Were it not for the leaping and twinkling of the soul, man would rot away in his greatest passion, idleness."

— Carl Gustav Jung, The Archetypes and the Collective Unconscious

Chapter 16 Archetypes

Interpreting the symbols in dreams helps with an understanding of archetypes. Carl Jung, a psychologist (1875 – 1961), is famous for his work on Archetypes.

As referenced by Conor Neill in his article "Understanding Personality: The 12 Jungian Archetypes."

Archetypes show up in many different areas.

- Platonic archetypes – Greek, Plato
- Jungian archetypes – Carl Jung
- Movies and Story archetypes – the Seven Basic plots
- Tarot
- Astrology
- Psychology
- Stereotypes

Jung defined 12 archetypes

1. Ruler
2. Creator/Artist
3. Sage
4. Innocent
5. Explorer

6. Rebel
7. Hero
8. Wizard
9. Jester
10. Everyman(person)
11. Lover
12. Caregiver

He then divided the archetypes into three different areas:

- Ego
- Self
- Soul

Further divided them into four classifications:

1. Personal - Leave a Mark on the World
2. Order -Provide Structure to the World
3. Social - Connect to others
4. Freedom - Yearn for Paradise

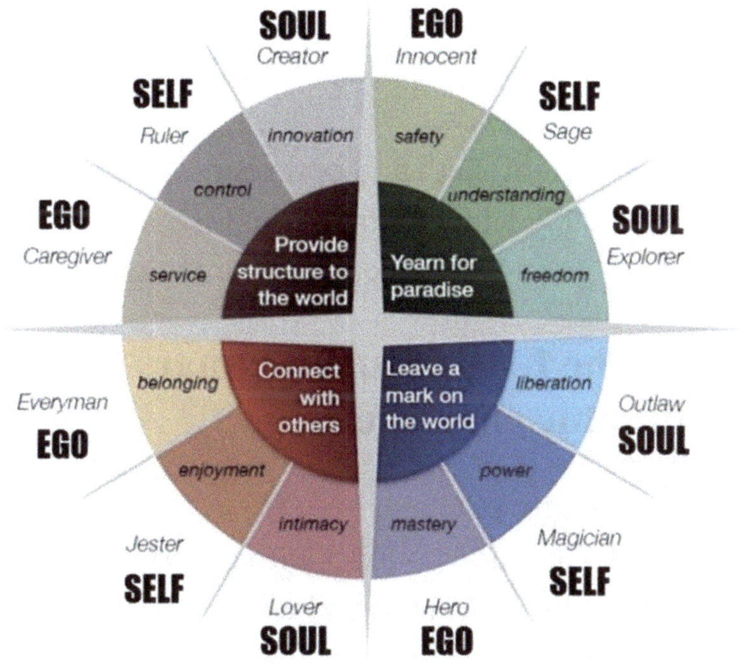

1. The Innocent

- Type: EGO
- Category: Yearn for paradise
- Motto: Free to be you and me
- Core desire: to get to paradise
- Goal: to be happy
- Greatest fear: to be punished for doing something bad or wrong

- Strategy: to do things right
- Weakness: boring for all their naive innocence
- Talent: faith and optimism
- AKA: Utopian, traditionalist, naive, mystic, saint, romantic, dreamer

2. The Everyman - ordinary and humble character

- Type: EGO
- Category: Connect with others
- Motto: All men and women are created equal
- Core Desire: connecting with others
- Goal: to belong
- Greatest fear: to be left out or to stand out from the crowd
- Strategy: develop ordinary solid virtues, be down to earth, and the common touch
- Weakness: losing one's self to blend in or for the sake of superficial relationships
- Talent: realism, empathy, lack of pretense

- AKA: The good old boy, regular guy/girl, the person next door, the realist, the working stiff, the solid citizen, the good neighbor, or the silent majority.

3. The Hero

- Type: EGO
- Category: Leave a Mark on the World
- Motto: Where there's a will, there's a way
- Core desire: to prove one's worth through courageous acts
- Goal: expert mastery in a way that improves the world
- Greatest fear: weakness, vulnerability, being a "chicken."
- Strategy: to be as strong and competent as possible
- Weakness: arrogance, always needing another battle to fight
- Talent: competence and courage
- AKA: The warrior, crusader, rescuer, superhero, soldier, dragon slayer, winner, and team player.

4. The Caregiver

- Type: EGO
- Category: Provide structure to the world
- Motto: Love your neighbor as yourself
- Core desire: to protect and care for others
- Goal: To help others
- Greatest fear: selfishness and ingratitude
- Strategy: doing things for others
- Weakness: martyrdom and being exploited
- Talent: compassion, generosity
- AKA: The Saint, altruist, parent, helper, or supporter.

5. The Explorer

- Type: Soul
- Category: Provide structure to the world
- Motto: Don't fence me in

- Core desire: the freedom to find out who you are through exploring the world
- Goal: to experience a better, more authentic, more fulfilling life
- Biggest fear: getting trapped, conformity, and inner emptiness
- Strategy: journey, seek out and experience new things, escape from boredom
- Weakness: aimless wandering, becoming a misfit
- Talent: autonomy, ambition, being true to one's soul
- AKA: The seeker, iconoclast, wanderer, individualist, or pilgrim.

6. The Outlaw / Rebel

- Type: Soul
- Category: Leave a mark on the world
- Motto: Rules are made to be broken
- Core desire: revenge or revolution
- Goal: to overturn what isn't working

- Greatest fear: to be powerless or ineffectual
- Strategy: disrupt, destroy, or shock
- Weakness: crossing over to the dark side, crime
- Talent: outrageousness, radical freedom
- AKA: The rebel, revolutionary, wild man, misfit, or iconoclast.

7. The Lover

- Type: Soul
- Category: Connect with others
- Motto: You're the only one
- Core desire: intimacy and experience
- Goal: being in a relationship with the people, work, and surroundings they love
- Greatest fear: being alone, a wallflower, unwanted, unloved
- Strategy: to become more and more physically and emotionally attractive
- Weakness: the outward-directed desire to please others at risk of losing own identity

- Talent: passion, gratitude, appreciation, and commitment
- AKA: The partner, friend, intimate, enthusiast, sensualist, spouse, or team-builder.

8. The Creator/Artist

- Type: Soul
- Category: Provide structure to the world
- Motto: If you can imagine it, it can be done
- Core desire: to create things of enduring value
- Goal: to realize a vision
- Greatest fear: mediocre vision or execution
- Strategy: develop artistic control and skill
- Task: to create culture, express ones vision
- Weakness: perfectionism, bad solutions
- Talent: creativity and imagination
- AKA: The artist, inventor, innovator, musician, writer, or dreamer.

9. The Jester

- Type: Self
- Category: Connect with others
- Motto: You only live once
- Core desire: to live in the moment with full enjoyment
- Goal: to have a great time and lighten up the world
- Greatest fear: being bored or boring others
- Strategy: play, make jokes, be funny
- Weakness: frivolity, wasting time
- Talent: joy
- AKA: The fool, trickster, joker, practical joker, or comedian.

10. The Sage

- Type: Self
- Category: Yearn for paradise
- Motto: The truth will set you free
- Core desire: to find the truth.

- Goal: to use intelligence and analysis to understand the world.
- Biggest fear: being duped, misled, or ignorant.
- Strategy: self-reflection and understanding thought processes; seeking out information and knowledge.
- Weakness: study details forever and never act.
- Talent: wisdom, intelligence.
- AKA: The expert, scholar, detective, advisor, thinker, philosopher, academic, researcher, thinker, planner, professional, mentor, teacher, or contemplative.

11. The Magician

- Type: Self
- Category: Leave a mark on the world
- Motto: I make things happen.
- Core desire: understanding the fundamental laws of the universe
- Goal: to make dreams come true

- Greatest fear: unintended negative consequences
- Strategy: develop a vision and live by it
- Weakness: becoming manipulative
- Talent: finding win-win solutions
- AKA: The visionary, catalyst, inventor, charismatic leader, shaman, healer, or medicine man.

12. The Ruler

- Type: Self
- Category: Provide structure to the world
- *Motto: Power isn't everything, it's the only thing.*
- *Core desire: control*
- *Goal: create a prosperous, successful family or community*
- *Strategy: exercise power*
- *Greatest fear: chaos, being overthrown*
- *Weakness: being authoritarian, unable to delegate*
- *Talent: responsibility, leadership*

- AKA: The boss, leader, aristocrat, king, queen, politician, role model, manager, or administrator.

In the world

Where do you fit in the archetypes? We all have aspects of each archetype, but we usually identify with one predominant archetype. Corporations align themselves with certain archetypes, as in the graphic below.

Chapter 16 Archetypes

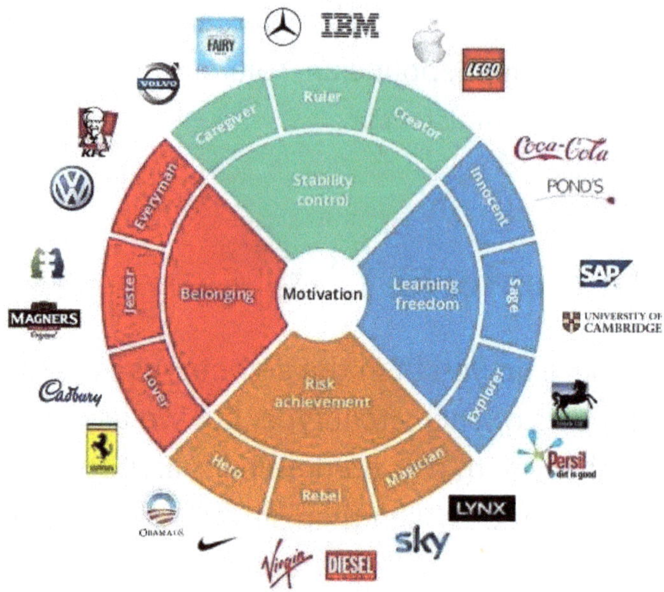

The Jung derived archetypes from the archetypes in the Tarot. I suggest getting a book on the Tarot and reading the meanings of the different cards. It is a fascinating look at the archetypes and life journeys we all take.

Chapter 16 Archetypes

Chapter 17 Controlling your Dreams

"[Lucid dreams help] you to progress on the path to self-mastery."

– Stephen LaBerge

Chapter 17 Controlling your Dreams

Being lucid and controlling your dreams is the ultimate goal. Controlling your dreams affects your subconscious mind, that part of you that interprets the dream. Controlling your dreams opens up new avenues of possibilities for the subconscious to flow into and will, at times, confuse the subconscious into a better resolution of the issue.

Controlling your dreams allows us to program dreams to accomplish many things. We can program and control dreams to learn new skills and new material.

One method of learning new material I used in college is studying while dreaming. The theory is that your subconscious mind remembers everything. Although our conscious mind sometimes has trouble with information recall. Let's suppose you have a chapter to read. Take a deliberate look at every page in the chapter, like you are taking a picture of the page. Stopping to get an image of each page. Then, when you go to sleep, say to yourself, "I will read (say the Chapter number and the title) while I sleep." You can also say I will read it two times or anything else you would like to add. Then, when you get up, read and study the chapter. I have vivid memories of dreams where I was reading the material; the next day, it was easier to absorb and understand when reading and studying the material.

You can do the same for reviewing your notes, practicing a sport, or learning new skills. Program your dreams for what you want, then work on those skills the next day. You still need to do the work, but it will be easier to learn and understand, accelerating your learning.

Chapter 17 Controlling your Dreams

Chapter 18 Triggers

"Lucid dreams show us the inner realities of existence which we have either been too busy or afraid to recognize."

— Michael Bassey Johnson, The Oneironaut's Diary

Chapter 18 Triggers

To accelerate your dreams, you can create triggers. In my class, I do a "Triggers" meditation. The purpose of the trigger is to condition your brain to act a certain way when you fire the trigger. It is like Pavlov's Dog. Ivan Pavlov, a psychologist, first showed how conditioned learning could cause a response. Pavlov did his experiments with dogs. A bell rang every time he dropped food into the dogs' feeding bowl. Then, after a time, he just rang the bell, and the dog salivated, expecting the food to be there.

We can use a trigger mechanism to condition ourselves to behave a certain way. Through guided meditation, I condition the use of touching the first two fingers of either hand to your forehead, just between your eyes at the third eye center. Touching your forehead will cause you to enter a lucid dream state. I am experimenting with this technique, and the results are promising. There is no reason we cannot cause ourselves to induce this state. In teaching the Silva Method, we use, what we call, the "Three-finger technique" to cause our minds to enter the alpha state to function better at that level of mind. This evidence supports using a trigger to enter lucid dreaming.

Chapter 18 Triggers

Chapter 19 Final Word

"You are what you do, not what you say you'll do."

— Carl Gustav Jung

Chapter 19 Final Word

Congratulations, you've made it this far. Now, it is time to practice and remember your dreams on a daily basis.

How to get started

Steps:

1. Read and study this book
2. Formulate your plan
3. Journal your dreams
4. Prioritize
5. Join the community at https://DreamSecrets.us
6. Register for the class
    a. There are supporting meditations in the online class
7. Connect with me and others
8. Report your success back to me

Chapter 20 Additional Resources

 https://alcy.com/readinglist recommended reading list

https://alcy.com is my general site with all my classes and training vault.

https://DreamSecrets.us is the site devoted to dreaming.

https://SilvaMethodKY.com I am a certified Silva Method Instructor. See this site for more information on the Silva Method.

Chapter 20 Additional Resources

Learn to Meditate: Techniques for the beginner and the experienced by Richard Siena, available on Amazon. Published Aug 31, 2020

Hashtag #RememberTheDream

 https://twitter.com/RichardSiena

 https://rumble.com/c/c-2194274

 https://linkedin.com/in/richardsiena

Chapter 21 References

The Art of Dreaming: A Creativity Toolbox for Dreamwork
By Jill Mellick, Marion Woodman

Lucid Dreaming, Plain and Simple: Tips and Techniques for Insight, Creativity, and Personal Growth
By Robert Waggoner, Caroline McCready

Lucid Dreaming: Gateway to the Inner Self
by Robert Waggoner

Lucid Dreaming: A Concise Guide to Awakening in Your Dreams and in Your Life
by Stephen LaBerge

The Chakras
by C.W. Leadbeater, Quest books, 1977 edition

Chapter 21 References

Understanding Personality: The 12 Jungian Archetypes

https://conorneill.com/2018/04/21/understanding-personality-the-12-jungian-archetypes/

The RA Material
By Don Elkins, Carla Rueckert, and James Allen McCarty

Beginner's guide to TAROT
By Juliet Sharman-Burke

Cover Design
Mohammad Akram

https://99designs.com/profiles/5576359/about

www.ingramcontent.com/pod-product-compliance
Lightning Source LLC
Chambersburg PA
CBHW070121100426
42744CB00010B/1893

* 9 7 8 1 7 3 5 6 3 8 4 2 3 *